Progress - not perfection

Sarah Anderson

Presentation by *BookLeaf Publishing*

Web: www.bookleafpub.com

E-mail: info@bookleafpub.com

ISBN: 9789357210430

First edition 2022

DEDICATION

this book is dedicated to Allison Tamney, who has always pushed me to better myself and is the definition of a true friend.

it is also dedicated to Catherine Thomas, who always ignites a creative flame within me and Curtis Turner, who loves me long time.

ACKNOWLEDGEMENT

i would like to express my gratitude to the transitions in my life, the subjects of the poetry, and BookLeaf Publishing for sparking this creativity and giving me an opportunity to express my emotion.

PREFACE

at any point in these works
if you believe a story is about you
it probably is

at any point in these works
if you believe a story expresses how you feel
take it and run with it

these are meant to be shared
these are meant to help
and these are meant to grow

HELLO

the world has been expecting you
bird songs, no longer in the background
its something you notice, wonder, recall
animals in general take on a new meaning
more than visitors, closer than neighbors, family

the world has been expecting you
sit down on the strong rock
warmed by the sun
see the possibilities that expand past the
mountain range
but also settle in the low valley

the world has been expecting you
surprise flight of a cricket will still make you
jump
no more a question of
"am I living my life right?"
pause, for a butterfly's graceful flight, your
reassurance

the world has been expecting you
remember the good before
remember the feeling that comes the with first
drops of rain

the taste of sweet honey suckle on a summers
day

this is exciting, difficult
but a good difficult
similar
but very different

no worries
don't over think
because the world has been expecting you

NATURE

no one tells nature what to be
it just is

right now i can hear the roar of the river
it does not care how loud it is
it does not lower its powerful sound for anyone

the trees group together
sometimes they provide shade
they do not ask if i'm comfortable
or if they need to slide over

a fly continues to land on my body
wherever it decides in that moment
there is no air traffic control
no asking permission

nature defines itself
it makes noise, creates habitats
and lands where it damn well pleases
there is nothing more it can give
it is already one hundred percent in front of us

QUESTIONS

how do we know it's the right thing?
am I really done?
or am I really scared?

challenges are what new situations bring
that can be seen by anyone
especially those who've cared

never could express feeling
spent most of the time trying to outrun
and pretend like they were never there

NASCAR

four left turns
there's etiquette
can't really say what it is
but i know there's a code

a staple in my life
that i didn't know i needed
or even wanted
small connection to the past

it's made me a winner
it's made me eager
and it's made smile
from four little words

gentlemen, start your engines.

FINE

you don't actually know
someone until
you live with them

dirty laundry get aired
both kinds
figurative and literal

you can ignore it
like we tried
or you can face it
head on

yes
i appreciate this about you
no
i can't handle this

i need help
i want to feel
wanted

chase after me
but let me continue

to run

dog, fine
cat, not super okay with dog
but fine
nonetheless

us
we're fine

we were
just fine

do we just ignore
and stay fine
for the rest of our lives

or do we burn this motherfucker down
with everything
we should have said
long before

ALL

don't understand how one
can be it all

watch what you eat
but treat yourself

don't need no man
but hey, if he's buying [that's a gentleman]

stay young, wild, free
but get yourself together, would ya?

constant pressures
contradictions

no way one person can be it all

SNAKE

i'm jealous of the snake
easily shedding its skin
discarded
left behind in the tall grass

the snake moves on
doesn't even look back
shiny, new exterior
predator once again

DRY

kindness and love all the way around.
how do you say what you want when you don't
actually know?
i've cried every day in the new year.
almost lost an ankle, but we're here.
you're anxious, but over it.
i was totally fine with this.
run as long as you want.
i'm going to be able to do it.
i don't want to be scared to move on.
i wanted more.
nothing is at all what i thought it would be like
and i'm slowly coming to realize that's okay.

PEANUTS

grief is not something i'm familiar with
but lately it's starting to feel like that annoying
neighbor
the one who feeds the squirrels
actual peanuts
only to have them come bury the shells in your
yard

at first you're frustrated
you buy a bee-bee gun
any squirrel that comes within 5ft of the house is
getting it
there's a new sheriff in town
and she's declaring peanuts illegal

one day you realize it's been months
peanut shells are popping up like crazy
the population had to have quadrupled
but you started this fight
and you're damn sure going to finish it

each day gets harder and harder
peanut shells higher and higher
for goodness sake...

where is the neighbor getting all these peanuts
i've never even seen him leave the house

the cat is losing it by the window
squirrels teasing her
dancing along the fence line
peanut in tow
and then something you never thought you'd say
comes out of your mouth

while recounting this story
about the annoying neighbor
and his army of squirrels
you call the king squirrel, "Mr. Peanuts"

mayday.
you have made a connection with the squirrel
frustration is fading
you actually say hello to the squirrels now
what are you doing solider?
fraternizing with the enemy

giving in.
because the neighbor can still afford giant bags
of peanuts
shells are continuing to pile up
you've now named all of Mr. Peanut's
grandchildren
you convince yourself you tried hard enough

it's time to either sell the house
or hope some of those were raw peanuts
and harvest them next year

ROOM

i saved a spot on my towel for you
beach sunrise, coffee [black]
not a cloud in the sky
not like before

cooler, louder, busier
it's amazing how time moves so quickly
one minute just a spectrum of colors across the
sky
the next a big ball of fire

flames and rays, engulfing the beach
as i slide over on the towel
7:04 | 7:09 | 7:12
closer to the middle i move
7:15 | 7:17
she's in the sky now, so perfect
and no one can tell her any different
7:18
you're not coming
but that's not why i'm here anymore

no more "i miss you"s
"i love you"s
good thing i always responded with "you don't"

i'm here for the salt, the sand
more importantly the sun
whose beauty is helping me recognize my own

and there's no more room for you on my towel

MOM

my new favorite thing
is when i call home
and mom picks up the phone

she says hello
in a singing voice
i always smile, never had a choice

we talk about our week
all the ups and downs
the gossip from both towns

she says, "you sound great"
we're one hundred miles apart
and my mom can still read my heart

never let it leave you

SMILE

keep smiling baby girl

your smile is your super power

share it with others

but most importantly

never let it leave you

WHOM

she moves to the beat of her own drum
somewhere out in left field they say
quick to fall in love
wants to be part of the solution
hides her own pain behind a glass of wine
knows there's more to her wild story
and looks forward to the entire ride

GROWTH

stop.
take a deep breath.
look at all you've done.
what you have accomplished.

focus on you.
not your neighbor.
honey, some would kill to be in your shoes.

this is rare.
recognizing your own growth.
be proud.
you were, and still are, the brave one.

CAR

sometimes
when i get home
i sit in my car
a little while

listen to a show
some music
scroll through social media
eat a snack

sometimes
i don't do anything
i sit in silence
stillness

both are good
for the heart
one helps you lose your mind
the other helps you find your soul

HONEY

it's been months
i'm happy & healthy
yet you still show up
if only for a second
rain the back, left corner
of my brain

that's your new home
it's a happy home
a healthy home
for both of us

it's filled with nostalgia
the smell of fresh cut grass
with an electric mower

avocado toast, bacon, eggs, mimosa
for brunch after an hour run

sounds from the latest dateline
or sports game in the background

with an American gothic picture
hanging in the hallway

you helped me see
that there could be a forever
& i will always love you for that

but your move to the back, left corner
of my brain
was inevitable
forever my fleeting treasure

DESERVE

love seeing you happy
you are glowing
whatever you are doing keep doing it
love this for you
you deserve this
yes honey
this is amazing
you're doing big things

everything you ever want to hear
when you're up
and you're happy

but where was this when i was down
i couldn't see an end
tell me
where were my friends

THERAPY

you cannot sit still
you always want the next big adventure
something always in the works
something to look forward to

keep that sense of wonder
keep that want for more
don't be afraid to slow down
don't worry where the dust settles

happiness can be found in spontaneity
happiness is also a warm blanket in the den
find joy in the possibilities the entire world gives
find joy in the possibilities your entire soul gives

JAMS

i've tried to write this
for a long time
it always starts with this:

"28 years.
10,365 days.
simultaneously existing."

i start with this
because when you use numbers
it is supposed to give a tangible value

i can't finish
what i want to say
because how do you sum up
a friendship
a legitimate
lifelong friendship

i'm trying with the numbers
the tangible value
the data holds me back, too

those are large numbers
but you can't put a value on us

you can't sum it up
it's so rare
and so perfect
in it's own way

i'm just so grateful
to be apart of this
for the 28 years.
10,365 days.
and counting…

FEELS

feels right
feels good
feels different than before

feels like butterflies
feels like sunrise
feels like my something more

feels like moving forward
feels like free falling
feels like excitement for what's in store

feels nice
feels warm
feels forevermore

BEAUTIFUL

i am not who i was yesterday
i am not who i will be in the future
each day, hour, minute brings new choices
new challenges
new experiences
that builds me
molds me
shapes me
in a never ending story
with words that combine ever so beautifully